THE STEVE WINWOOD KEYBOARD SONGBOOK

SPENCER DAVIS GROUP • TRAFFIC • BLIND FAITH • STEVE WINWOOD

Produced by
Alfred Music Publishing Co., Inc.
P.O. Box 10003
Van Nuys, CA 91410-0003
alfred.com

Printed in USA.

ISBN-10: 0-7390-7596-9
ISBN-13: 978-0-7390-7596-8

 Alfred Cares. Contents printed on 100% recycled paper.

CONTENTS

SONG	ARTIST	PAGE
Back in the High Life Again	Steve Winwood	84
Can't Find My Way Home	Blind Faith	65
Dear Mr. Fantasy	Traffic	16
Dirty City	Steve Winwood	98
Empty Pages	Traffic	21
The Finer Things	Steve Winwood	106
Freedom Rider	Traffic	30
Gimme Some Lovin'	Spencer Davis Group	4
Glad	Traffic	36
Had to Cry Today	Blind Faith	57
Higher Love	Steve Winwood	91
I'm a Man	Spencer Davis Group	8
The Low Spark of High-Heeled Boys	Traffic	41
Pearly Queen	Traffic	50
Presence of the Lord	Blind Faith	78
Roll with It	Steve Winwood	113
Valerie	Steve Winwood	124
Well All Right	Blind Faith	73
While You See a Chance	Steve Winwood	118

SPENCER DAVIS GROUP

GIMME SOME LOVIN'

Words and Music by
STEVE WINWOOD, MUFF WINWOOD
and SPENCER DAVIS

Moderately fast ♩ = 148

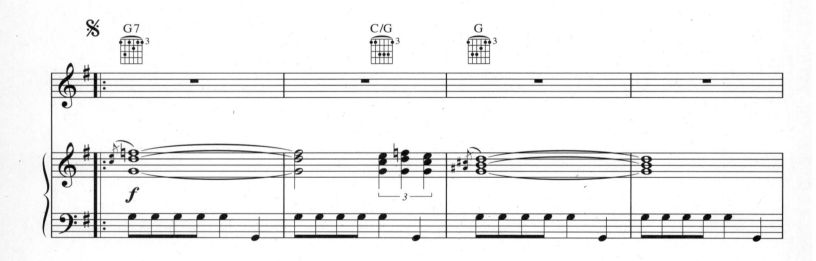

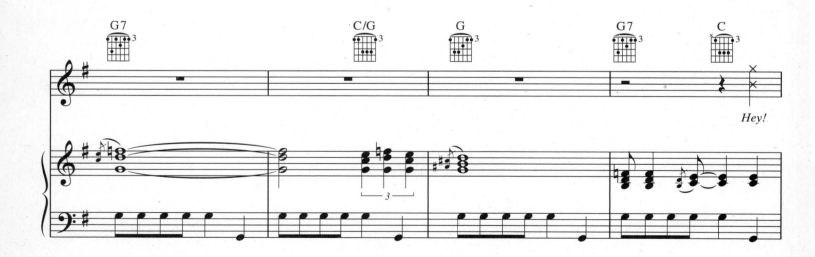

Hey!

Gimme Some Lovin' - 4 - 1

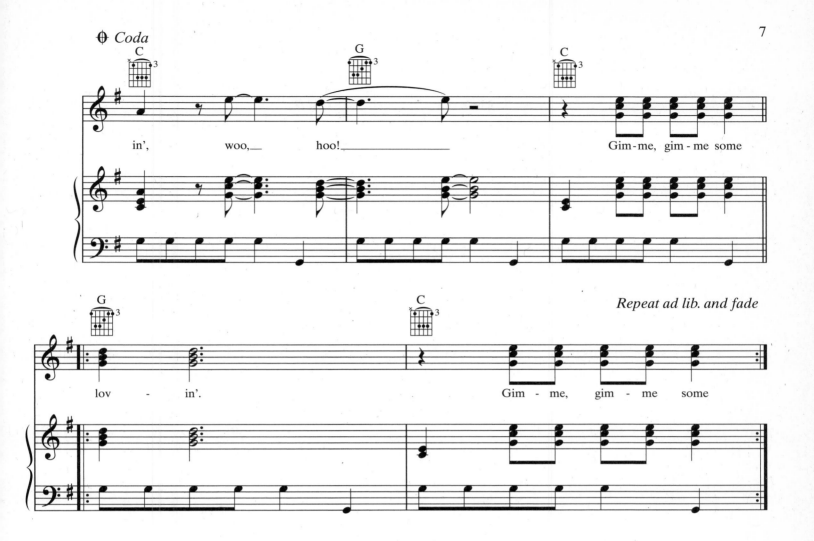

Coda

in', woo, hoo! Gim-me, gim-me some

lov - in'. Gim - me, gim - me some

Repeat ad lib. and fade

Verse 2:
Well, I feel so good, everything is sounding hot.
You better take it easy 'cause the place is on fire.
Been a hard day and I don't know what to do.
Wait a minute, baby, it could happen to you.
And I'm so glad we made it, so glad we made it.
(To Chorus:)

Verse 3:
Well, I feel so good, everybody's gettin' high.
You better take it easy 'cause the place is on fire.
Been a hard day, nothing went too good.
Now I'm gonna relax, honey, everybody should.
And I'm so glad we made it, so glad we made it.
(To Chorus:)

I'M A MAN

Words and Music by
STEVE WINWOOD and JIMMY MILLER

I'm a Man - 7 - 1

12

Verse 3:

I'm a Man - 7 - 5

I'm a Man - 7 - 7

TRAFFIC

DEAR MR. FANTASY

Words and Music by
STEVE WINWOOD, CHRIS WOOD
and JIM CAPALDI

Verses 1 & 3:

1.3. Dear Mis-ter Fan - ta-sy, play us a tune,_____ some-thing to make_ us all__ hap-

py._____ Do an - y - thing,_ take_ us out of this_ gloom._____ Sing a song,_

⊕ *Coda*

Instrumental solo ad lib.:

Play 5 times

Repeat and fade

EMPTY PAGES

Words and Music by
STEVE WINWOOD

Empty Pages - 9 - 1

Verses 2 & 3:

2. She's the one,____ makes me feel____ so good____
3. Of - ten lost____ and for - got - ten.

when ev - 'ry-thing is a - gainst__ me. Picks me up____ when I'm feel -
Her weak - ness and____ the mud._____ I've been think - ing I'm work -

ing bad,____ so I____ got some-thing to show._____ }
ing too hard,_ but I____ got some-thing to show._____ }

Chorus:

Star - ing at emp - ty pag - es, cen - tered 'round_ the

ƒ (E.P. and Organ)

24

Empty Pages - 9 - 5

Do do do____ do do do____ do do,____

28

FREEDOM RIDER

Words and Music by
STEVE WINWOOD and JIM CAPALDI

Freedom Rider - 6 - 1

32 **Tempo I**

Freedom Rider - 6 - 3

Freedom Rider - 6 - 4

GLAD

Words and Music by
STEVE WINWOOD

Moderately fast ♩ = 132

(Tenor sax. melody):

Glad - 5 - 1

40

Additional organ and piano solos (ad lib.):
Solo 2: Organ, 28 measures
Solo 3: Piano, 16 measures

Glad - 5 - 5

THE LOW SPARK OF HIGH-HEELED BOYS

Words and Music by
STEVE WINWOOD and JIM CAPALDI

Repeat as desired

Moderately ♩ = 108

gradual fade in

Verse:

see some-thing that looks like a star,____ and it's shoot-ing up out of the ground,____
you had just a min-ute to breathe,____ and they grant-ed you one fi-nal wish,____
give you ev-'ry-thing that I own____ and ask for noth-ing in re-turn,____

The Low Spark of High-Heeled Boys - 9 - 1

And the thing that you're hear - ing is on - ly the sound of the low_
And the thing that dis - turbs_ you is on - ly the sound of the low_
And the sound that I'm hear - ing is on - ly the sound of the low_

_ spark of high - heeled boys._
_ spark of high - heeled boys._
_ spark of high - heeled boys._

Chorus:

Mmm._

The per - cent - age you're pay - ing is too_ high priced,_ while you're

46

The Low Spark of High-Heeled Boys - 9 - 6

Repeat ad lib. and fade

PEARLY QUEEN

Words and Music by
STEVE WINWOOD and JIM CAPALDI

3. I had a

5. I trav - el

Verse 5:

'round the world___ to find the sun. I could-n't stop my - self___ from

BLIND FAITH

HAD TO CRY TODAY

Words and Music by
STEVE WINWOOD

Had to cry_____ to - day._____

CAN'T FIND MY WAY HOME

All gtrs. in Drop D tuning:
⑥ = D   ③ = G
⑤ = A   ② = B
④ = D   ① = E

Words and Music by
STEVE WINWOOD

Verse 1:

down   off__ your   throne_____   and   leave   your   bod-y a - lone._____

Can't Find My Way Home - 8 - 1

WELL ALL RIGHT

Words and Music by
JERRY ALLISON, BUDDY HOLLY,
JOE MAUDLIN and NORMAN PETTY

Moderate country-rock ♩ = 108

1. Well all right,_

(sample bass line)

Repeat ad lib. and fade

Well All Right - 5 - 5

PRESENCE OF THE LORD

Words and Music by
ERIC CLAPTON

Presence of the Lord - 5 - 1

Double time ♩ = 120

Guitar solo ad lib.:

N.C.

Tempo I (♩ = 60)

D.S. 𝄋 al Coda

⊕ *Coda*

in___ the col - our of the

Lord._____

rit.

STEVE WINWOOD

BACK IN THE HIGH LIFE AGAIN

Words and Music by
STEVE WINWOOD and WILL JENNINGS

Verse 1 (sing 1st time only):

used to seem_ to me that my life ran on_ too fast, and I

Verse 2 (sing 2nd time only):

used to be_ the best to make life be life_ to me, and I

Back in the High Life Again - 7 - 1

90

Begin fade

Fade out

HIGHER LOVE

Words and Music by
STEVE WINWOOD and WILL JENNINGS

Higher Love - 7 - 1

Play 2nd time only

Things look so bad ev - 'ry - where._

In this whole world, what is fair? We walk blind_ and we

try to see,____ fall - ing be - hind in what could be.

94

Bridge:

I could light the night up with my soul on fire.

I could make the sun shine from pure de-sire. Let me feel that

love come o - ver me. Let me feel how strong it could be.

N.C.

Oh.

Higher Love - 7 - 7

DIRTY CITY

Gtr. tuned "drop D":
⑥ = D

Words and Music by
STEVE WINWOOD and PETER GODWIN

Slow sixteenth-note groove ♩ = 63

Dirty City - 8 - 1

100

looked in his room when I___ got home and un-der-neath the cov-ers found_ load-ed_
roar of the train runs by___ my room and on these sum-mer nights_ I can't_ sleep_ an-y-

gun._____ He
more._____ I

looked at me with emp-ty eyes, he said, "It's time for me__ to be__ mov-in'_
walk in the streets to greet_ the dawn or stay at home all night_ and stare_ at___ the__

on."_____
floor._____

Chorus:

104

THE FINER THINGS

Words and Music by
STEVE WINWOOD and WILL JENNINGS

Moderately ♩ = 130

(with pedal)

Moderate reggae feel

Chorus:

The fin - er things keep shin - ing through,__ the way my soul gets

lost__ in you.__ The fin - er things I feel__ in me.__

The gold - en dance life could__ be.__ 2. I've been sad,__

ROLL WITH IT

Words and Music by
STEVE WINWOOD, WILL JENNINGS,
EDDIE HOLLAND, LAMONT DOZIER
and BRIAN HOLLAND

Roll With It - 5 - 1

114

Roll With It - 5 - 2

WHILE YOU SEE A CHANCE

Words and Music by
STEVE WINWOOD and WILL JENNINGS

Slowly and freely

(Synth.)

Moderately ♩ = 126

While You See a Chance - 6 - 1

Verses 1 & 4:

1.4. Stand up in a clear___ blue morn - ing, un - til___ you see_____ what can be;_

VALERIE

Words and Music by
STEVE WINWOOD and WILL JENNINGS

Lyrics: I'm the same boy I used to be.___